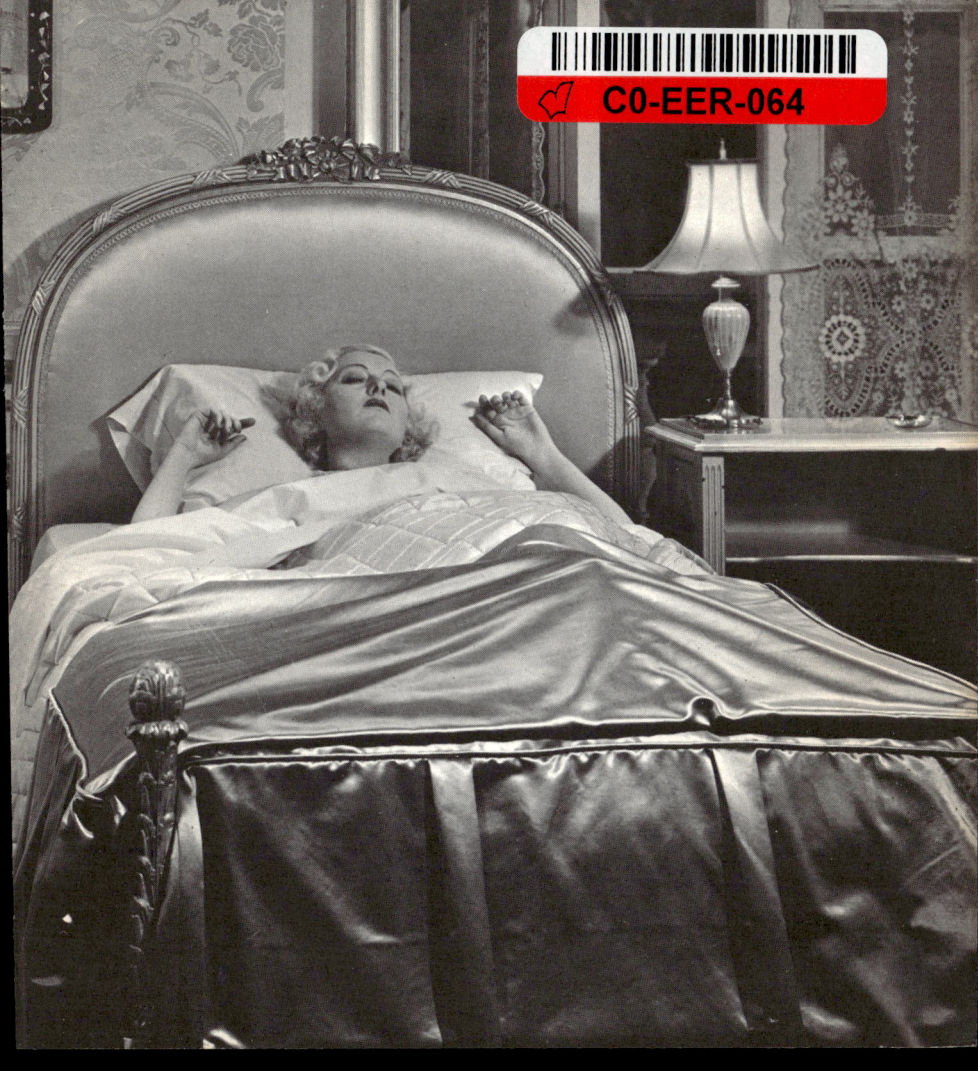

Fields' Day

The Best of W.C.Fields

Photographs: Culver Pictures, cover, end papers, 2, 5, 7, 8, 14, 17, 19, 20, 23, 24; R. R. Stuart Collection, title page, 11, 12, back cover. Copyright © 1972 by Hallmark Cards, Inc., Kansas City, Missouri. All Rights Reserved. Printed in the United States of America. Library of Congress Catalog Card Number: 70-175035. Standard Book Number: 87529-266-6.

Your kid looks like a monkey.

Damnation, the perfume you're wearing is intoxic.

Drat! Someone's been putting pineapple juice in my pineapple juice.

I'll make her a lady if I have to knock her down to do it.

Hmmmm. All dressed up like an open grave.

I didn't make disparaging remarks about your steak. I merely said that
I hadn't seen that old horse that you used to keep outside around here lately!

I'd rather have two girls at 21 each than one girl at 42.

I never smoked a thing before I was nine.

It ain't a fit night out for man nor beast!

Some weasel took the cork out
of my lunch!

Ah, the patter of little feet around
the house. There's nothing like having
a midget for a butler.

My heart is a bargain today.
Will you take it?

Your line is "goo, goo." Don't muff it.

There may be some things better than sex, and some things may be worse, but there is nothing exactly like it.

Either you're drunk or your braces are lopsided.

I'd like to see Paris before I die-- Philadelphia will do.

Don't cry and I'll let you smell my breath.

Anything worth having is worth cheating for.

Great stars! It's the chamber pot that's been missing from my chamber.

We lost our corkscrew and were compelled to live on food and water for several days.

Is he one of a kind or part of a matched set?

Ah, your lips are like tiny little
wine presses.

Sleep--the most beautiful experience
in life--except drink!

Stay in this room and don't fall out the
window unless it's absolutely necessary.

I think I'll go out and milk the elk.

I never drink anything stronger than gin before breakfast.

He had a nasty fall. I think it scrambled his adenoids.

We'll spend the weekend hunting chicken livers, yellow breasted chicken livers.

Don't wait up for me my dear. I may play a little parcheesi.

Later I'll take you outside and let you ride piggy back on a buzz saw.

I'm not given to rash statements, but either he goes or I go with him.

Lay out my semi-precious watch chain.

Cross my heart and hope to eat my weight in goslings.

I've been drinking professionally since I was 10...I was a backward child.

You can't hurt a child dropping him on his head. At that age their heads are soft anyway.

She was wearing a wig, but there was no accounting for her teeth.

Don't worry, my love. It's only a head cold. I don't plan to be out of work for more than six months.

How can you possibly hurt a watch by dipping it in molasses? It just makes me love the little nipper all the more!

Why, I've never struck a woman in my whole life, not even my own mother!

Ah, my sweet, your eyes are like linseed pools.

I want to look as spiffy as a penguin.
On second thought, a penguin in
sports clothes.

She was built like a brick chickenhouse.

Some of my best friends are bandits...
the president of the bank comes up
to my house!

Is this your basketball? It seems to have
fallen under my tire several times.

On the whole,
I'd rather have been in Philadelphia.